The Hundred and One Dalmatians

by Dodie Smith

Adapted for the stage by

Glyn Robbins

Samuel French — London
New York - Toronto - Hollywood

CHARACTERS

Missis Pongo, a Dalmatian lady dog
Pongo, a Dalmatian dog
Mr Dearly, their human pet
Mrs Dearly, their pet's wife
Nanny Cook
Nanny Butler
Mrs Cruella de Vil
Persian Cat
James-Or-Whoever
Perdita, a lady dog
Lucky
Cadpig } Dalmatian Puppies
Patch
Roly-Poly
A Policeman
A Golden Retriever
A Human Child
A Man
A Spaniel
Saul Baddun
Jasper Baddun
Sir Charles
Lieutenant Cat
Colonel Sheepdog
A Staffordshire Bull Terrier, with an East London accent
Billie Driver, a removal consultant
Street Denizens, **Servants**, many more small **Dalmatians**

THE HUNDRED AND ONE DALMATIANS

First presented at the Sherman Theatre, Cardiff on 29th November, 1995 with the following cast of characters:

Pongo	Simon Armstrong
Missis Pongo	Erica Eirian
Cruella de Vil	Helen Griffin
Mr Dearly	Robert Lane
Mrs Dearly	Kathryn Dimery
Butler	Eiry Thomas
Cook	Lynne Seymour
Spaniel	Kathryn Dimery
Sir Charles	Robert Lane
Saul	Eiry Thomas
Jasper	Lynne Seymour
Colonel	Robert Lane
Billie	Kathryn Dimery
Perdita	Eiry Thomas
Retriever	Lynne Seymour
Cat	Kathryn Dimery
Terrier	Robert Lane

The parts of Lucky and other Dalmatians, Street Denizens and others were played by local volunteers

Directed by Phil Clark

THE HUNDRED AND ONE DALMATIANS

Presented by Vanessa Ford Productions at the Theatre Royal, Bath with the following cast of characters:

Missis Pongo	Claire Nicholson
Pongo	Anthony Renshaw
Mr Dearly	Jason Griffiths
Mrs Dearly	Caroline O'Neill
Nanny Cook	Julian James
Nanny Butler	Alison Ridgeway
Mrs Cruella de Vil	Victoria Plum
Persian Cat	Nick Fordham
James-Or-Whoever	James Boston
Perdita	Alison Ridgeway
A Policeman	James Boston
A Golden Retriever	Timothy Marsh
A Spaniel	Nick Fordham
Saul Baddun	Julian James
Jasper Baddun	James Boston
Sir Charles	Jason Griffiths
Lieutenant Cat	Caroline O'Neill
Colonel Sheepdog	Nick Fordham
A Staffordshire Bull Terrier	Jason Griffiths
Billie Driver	Timothy Marsh

The parts of Lucky and other Dalmatians, Street Denizens and others were played by local volunteers

Directed by Phil Clark

SYNOPSIS OF SCENES

SUGGESTED CASTING /DOUBLING

Actor 1 Mrs Cruella de Vil
Actor 2 Missis
Actor 3 Pongo
Actor 4 Mrs Dearly/Lieutenant Cat
Actor 5 Mr Dearly/Sir Charles
Actor 6 Nanny Butler/ Saul Baddun
Actor 7 Nanny Cook/Jasper Baddun/Policeman
Actor 8 Persian Cat/A Spaniel/Colonel Sheepdog
Actor 9 James-Or-Whoever/A Golden Retriever
Others: Lucky; a Human Child; Dalmatians; Street Denizens

PRODUCTION NOTE

Both Dodie Smith and Glyn Robbins subscribe to the thesis that while dogs
and other animals are perfectly capable of understanding almost everything
humans say, the reverse is nowhere near true. It may be helpful to suggest that
in the play animals may stand on two legs unless humans are present.

SETTINGS

There are just a few things to remember that may make designing the settings
much easier. The Dearlys and the de Vils live on the same edge of Regent's
Park — so their rooms can be similar in style, but not in finish. That looks after
the bulk of Act I.

Most of Act II takes place in the forests of Essex and Suffolk, which could
appear similar. The Sudbury Manor scene requires intimacy — so the focus
should be on the fireplace, armchairs, and tea necessities — rather than the
interior. Hell Hall can be empty but for a television set, a light bulb holder and
its inhabitants.

There are so many ways the play could be tackled: revolves, split staging,
use of cloths and gauzes — all depending upon ingenuity, financial bound-
aries, and current fashion. The greatest of these is ingenuity.

This play is dedicated to
Laurence Fitch, Vanessa Ford, Alexander Ford-Robbins
and to the cardiac transplant team at Papworth Hospital,
particularly Dr Peter M. Schofield, Cathy Stewart, Dr Chris Green,
Dr Andrew Parry, Dr Keith McNeill,
Mr S. Nashen and Dr Jayan Parameshwar.
Without their skill, friendship and support it could not have been.

Other adaptations by Glyn Robbins
published by Samuel French Ltd

The Narnia novels by C. S. Lewis:
The Horse and his Boy
The Lion, the Witch and the Wardrobe
The Magician's Nephew
The Voyage of the Dawn Treader

The novel by A. A. Milne:
Winnie-the-Pooh

ACT I

Regent's Park, London. Late afternoon

When the CURTAIN *rises, some Denizens are walking their dogs; others, including Mr and Mrs Dearly, are merely promenading. Mrs Dearly is carrying parcels. A car-horn sounds very stridently, and we notice in the distance what looks like a black and white striped car, which the Dearlys approach, Mrs Dearly excitedly, Mr Dearly cautiously. The Dog Walkers demand our attention as we are taken to:*

SCENE 1

The dining-room of the Dearlys' house on the edge of Regent's Park, London. 5 p.m.

We are in a large room that contains a cupboard, a dining-table and chairs, a butler's table, a serving hatch or lift, a telephone

A clock strikes 5.00 p.m. Missis Pongo, a pregnant Dalmatian, is reclining, asleep, on the carpet

Pongo, her dog, barks off

Pongo enters. He is upright and walks over to her on two legs

She wakes up. They greet each other

Missis Oh, it's you. Are there any pets about, Pongo?

Pongo No, my dear. Cook and Butler are below stairs having a talk. And the Dearlys aren't home yet. But how are you feeling? You are taking care, aren't you? Can I get you anything?

Missis Thank you, no. You are so good to me, so understanding. Not like pets.

Pongo They try. They try very hard, some of them. And our pets are really very nice. And very concerned about you.

Missis But they still think that *they* own *us*.

Pongo The ones that love us always get it the wrong way round. It's quite amusing really. And our Mr and Mrs Dearly are fairly intelligent at least.

Missis They're intelligent?

Pongo Well, they understand quite a bit of our language: "Out, please!" "In, please!" "What about a walk?"

Missis "Hurry up with my dinner!" Yes, I suppose so.

Pongo And sometimes they even understand looks, or a paw scratch on the floor.

Missis Yes, I suppose so. No, I think we're lucky. And our puppies will be, too, my dear. Now, perhaps you ought to go and rest somewhere else. The pets will be needing the dining-room for their dinner.

Missis Someone's coming. It sounds like Butler.

Pongo Heading for the front door. The Dearlys arriving home, perhaps? (*He goes down on four legs and points expectantly*) Well, I'm ready for them.

The sound of a heavy front door opening. Squeaks of people coming into the house

Missis gets up on four legs, heavily

Missis I'm ready, too, dear.

Mr Dearly enters wearing street-clothes

Mr Dearly And will you get Cook up here too, please Nanny Butler. A full family conference is required. Hallo, Pongo. How are you, boy?

Pongo (*happily*) Wuffo!

Mr Dearly And Missis Pongo! Nothing's happened yet, I see. But it will, it will, my girl!

Missis Wuff.

Mrs Dearly enters, also wearing street clothes

Mr Dearly You've unloaded your parcels, my dear. Excellent. Now, where are Cook and Butler? Ah! Here we are.

Nanny Cook and Nanny Butler enter

Now, dear wife, would you care to explain?

Nanny Cook If it's about dinner, ma'am ...

Mrs Dearly Yes, it is about dinner. We have invited a guest.

Nanny Cook		
Nanny Butler	(*together*)	A guest?
Pongo		West?

Nanny Butler That's a bit sudden, ma'am.

Mrs Dearly Well, it all happened rather suddenly, you see. We were walking home when we heard an extremely loud motor-horn. It was really very loud ...

Mr Dearly The car was stopped at a house just ahead of us.

Mrs Dearly Then I saw this extremely tall wom —— er, lady, at the wheel of the car.

Mr Dearly Then she got out.

Nanny Cook What was she wearing?

Mrs Dearly She was wearing a very tight-fitting emerald satin dress, several ropes of rubies, and an absolutely simple white mink cloak. And she had ruby-red high-heeled shoes.

Mr Dearly She looked completely stunning. Dark skin, deep black eyes, and her hair — her hair was so unusual.

Mrs Dearly And when I saw her hair, I realized who she was. It was Cruella de Vil. We were at school together. Only, she was expelled for drinking ink.

Nanny Butler She sounds a bit, well a bit showy to me.

Mrs Dearly She always was. But we just had to talk, didn't we. And she asked how we were and where we were living. And I told her all about this house and the dogs, and we asked her and her husband round for dinner. Tonight.

Nanny Butler
Nanny Cook } (*together*) Tonight?
Pongo
Missis

Nanny Butler That is somewhat sudden, madam.

Mr Dearly Well, we didn't ask her, she sort of asked herself if you know what I mean. And the husband won't be dining with us. He's got work to do at one of their farms.

Mrs Dearly She'll be here very soon. So, Nanny Butler, can you lay the table for three, please. Nanny Cook, what were we having for dinner?

Nanny Cook Well, ma'am. I had planned French game pie, that's a pie of veal, pork, pheasant, partridge, bacon, truffles, spices and ——

Mrs Dearly It sounds perfect. And what about vegetables? Hors d'oeuvres? Entrée? Dessert? Cruella is very fussy about her food. I remember from school.

Nanny Cook Well, I could always give you the full ten courses. How about truite saumonée, sauce l'ermitage, followed by côte du boeuf rôti avec pommes macaire. Then timbale de ris de veau aux petits pois and terrine Brillat-Savarin. Of course, I'd need a little more warning, a little more notice ...

Mr Dearly I'm sure everything will be in apple-pie order, my dear. Just leave it up to Cook.

Nanny Butler And in the meantime I had better prepare the table.
Mrs Dearly While we go and get properly dressed. Quickly, my dear.

Mr and Mrs Dearly exit

Nanny Butler starts to lay the table for three. Nanny Cook helps her

Nanny Cook And speaking of proper dress I still think you're wrong about yours. A black dress with a frilly apron would be much more proper.
Nanny Butler A dress would be totally wrong. You can't be a butler without trousers.

The sound of a strident car-horn

Nanny Cook I wish you'd follow my advice. A frilly apron would really suit you.
Nanny Butler Actually, I followed your advice and bought one. It's over here somewhere. See? I agree with you, and besides it adds a touch of originality.

The front doorbell. The dogs bark and point

Nanny Cook Oh, no, there's the bell. I'd better make myself scarce.

Nanny Cook exits

Nanny Butler And I'd better go and answer it. I'll just check the table.

The doorbell rings again impatiently. The dogs bark again

Quiet, you two. (*Calling out*) Coming!

Nanny Butler exits

Missis That Cruella de Vil sounds a bit of a problem to me.
Pongo What makes you say that?
Missis Butler and Mrs Dearly didn't like the way she dressed. And the woman's very fussy about her food. She sounds like a cat.
Pongo That's not fair.
Missis And what about that horrible motor-horn? Anyone who has a motor-horn like that is a real show-off.
Pongo Watch out! Humans!

Mr and Mrs Dearly enter

Mr Dearly And this is the dining-room. Where we will be dining tonight.
Mrs Dearly Do come in, Cruella.

Cruella enters, draped in a white mink cloak. Her lengthy hair is distinctive, in that one side is white, the other black

Mr Dearly Which raises a most important point. How do I address you?
Cruella As Cruella, of course. Actually, my surname is still de Vil. I am the last of my family so I made my husband change his name to mine. Of course. He is known now as Mr de Vil. A matter *you* must explain to *me*, however, is how it is you come to have a female butler working for you called Nanny. It's so — well so, modern.
Mr Dearly We also have another — Nanny Cook!
Cruella My dears — how advanced!
Mrs Dearly Not really, Cruella. Their surnames were Cook and Butler and they used to be our nannies. When we got married, our dogs and our nannies moved in with us. It seemed a most sensible arrangement.
Cruella Sensible and practical. What is it you do for the Government?
Mrs Dearly Dearly has done the Government a great service. (*Proudly*) He is called a wizard of finance.
Cruella But then so many are, my dear.

The mink cloak slips to the floor. Mr Dearly picks it up

Mr Dearly What a beautiful cloak. But you'll find it too warm in here.
Cruella I never find anything too warm. I wear furs all the year round. Indeed, I sleep between ermine sheets.
Mrs Dearly How nice. Do they wash well?
Cruella I worship furs. I live for furs. That's why I married a furrier.
Mr Dearly Your husband's a furrier?

Pongo and Missis growl

Cruella Those must be the two delightful Dalmatian dogs you were telling me about.
Mr Dearly This is Pongo and this is Missis.

Pongo and Missis woof politely

Mrs Dearly They're expecting puppies.
Cruella Oh are they? Good! Come here, dogs.

Pongo and Missis do. They try to make friends with Cruella and both end up sneezing

What absolutely beautiful dogs. Wouldn't they make enchanting fur coats. For spring wear, over a black suit.

Pongo barks menacingly

Mrs Dearly It was only a joke, Pongo, dear. You know, sometimes I think the dogs understand every word we say.

Pongo }
Missis } *(together)* We do.

Cruella *(laughing)* Oh, that's ridiculous.

Mr Dearly Now, about dinner.

Mrs Dearly We have planned French game pie and ——

Cruella Oh, I am so sorry. I know I said I could make it for dinner tonight but I'd forgotten, until I looked in my engagement diary, that I'd already accepted an invitation from somebody else. So I'm afraid I can't dine with you tonight, but you must certainly dine with me tomorrow. Will that be all right? Oh, good. Now I must go, I'm afraid. Lovely, lovely dogs. They'd go so well with my striped black and white car. That's food for thought, isn't it?

Cruella exits

Mrs Dearly I'll see Cruella out, dear. You could go down and deal with Nanny Cook. And tell her about tomorrow.

Mrs Dearly exits

Mr Dearly Thank you so much, my dear. Well, I suppose the dogs would really enjoy some French game pie. After all, they are hunting dogs, aren't they?

Mr Dearly exits

The dogs bark after him

Missis We are most certainly not hunting dogs. We are coach or carriage dogs.

From outside, the sound of a very loud car-horn and a car driving off

Pongo Now then, you mustn't get upset. You remember what the Splendid Veterinary Surgeon Man said about that.

Missis Yes, I do. But he doesn't have to deal with humans. (*She sets off exploring*)

Pongo That's not strictly true, my dear. What are you doing?

Missis I'm exploring. I'm looking for boxes. What do you think I'm doing?

Pongo Looking for boxes? In here? Oh, crikey! The first sign of puppies!

Missis Do you think I might find some in this cupboard? Help me. Give me a paw.

Pongo Oh, dogbaskets! I was told about this. Puppies are on the way! (*He barks for help three times*)

Missis What are you doing barking for help? Just lend me your paw.

Mr Dearly enters

Mr Dearly I heard you call. What's wrong, Pongo?

Pongo is pointing towards Missis who is rooting around the cupboard

Pongo Wuffboard! Wuppies! *Wuppies!*

Mr Dearly I understand, Pongo. Now, we must get her outside to the broom cupboard. It's all prepared and ready for her. No brooms, just a nice comfortable box.

Missis Wuffbox?

Mr Dearly That's right — a lovely soft blanket in a big roomy box, all set up just for you. Follow me, Missis Pongo. No, not you, Pongo. Now don't look hurt. It's best at a time like this that she be left alone. We'll take good care of her, don't you worry. Come on, Missis.

Mr Dearly and Missis exit

Pongo is left on his own, pacing unhappily round the room

Pongo I just hope she has a nice easy time. After all, it is her first — our first family. I wonder how many there will be.

The sound of a strident car-horn, then the doorbell

Not too many, I hope, because then we might all be able to stay together. Like a proper family. Still, it doesn't really matter, as long as she's all right.

Cruella de Vil enters, wearing now a black satin dress with ropes of pearls and the white mink cloak. She is followed by Mrs Dearly

Cruella (*laughing*) So, you see my dear, he had got it totally wrong in my engagement diary as usual. The other invitation was for next week. I looked so silly when they told me — and then I remembered your oh-so-kind invitation and thought the proper thing to do was to come straight back here and accept it. Delicious French game pie, I seem to remember. With plenty of pepper, I hope.

Mrs Dearly Pepper?

Cruella Yes, pepper. I simply can't get enough pepper. I take pepper for breakfast with my toast, of course; with my lunch, naturally; with my afternoon tea and biscuits — doesn't everyone? My favourite of all and everything is pepper with my fruit salad.

Mrs Dearly I'll tell Butler. (*She rings*)

Nanny Butler enters immediately

My goodness, you were quick.

Nanny Butler Was I? Ladies, I came to tell you that the puppies are arriving earlier than expected. Which will of course delay dinner. Mr Dearly has asked you to remember that Missis has never before been a mother. She requires absolute quiet.

Cruella screeches. Pongo barks

Nanny Butler exits

Cruella Puppies? Arriving? Where are those puppies? I must see the little darlings.

Cruella exits

Mrs Dearly is stroke-calming Pongo

Mrs Dearly Missis will be all right, Pongo. You mustn't worry. Everybody wants to help her. She's surrounded by friends. The puppies are in good hands.

Cruella enters

Cruella Well, that was a big disappointment.

Pongo reacts

Mrs Dearly What's happened? Is Missis all right?

Cruella Of course she is. But the puppies aren't.

Pongo reacts again

Mrs Dearly Why what's wrong with them?
Cruella They're mongrels. They can't possibly be his puppies. You must drown them at once. They've got no spots at all. They're just white all over.
Mrs Dearly Cruella, Dalmatian dogs are always born white.

Pongo expresses relief and incredulity at Cruella's ignorance

The spots come later. And we wouldn't drown them even if they were mongrels.
Cruella Oh, it's quite easy, my dear. I've drowned dozens and dozens of my cat's kittens. She always chooses some wretched alley-cat to be their father — so her kittens are never worth keeping. Drowning's all they're fit for.
Mrs Dearly Surely, you leave her one kitten?
Cruella No, if I did that we'd be overrun with small cats. Are you absolutely sure those horrid little white rats, those so-called puppies, are really Dalmatians?

Pongo is not amused

How long will it be before they are old enough to leave their mother? In case I want to buy some?
Mrs Dearly Seven or eight weeks. And I have to talk with Mr Dearly to see if we want to put any up for sale. Well, we won't be getting dinner for a long while now — so perhaps you'd better go back home. This way.
Cruella Seven or eight weeks, eh? That's a bit longer than I thought. I was thinking tomorrow or the next day.
Mrs Dearly Come on, Cruella. This way out.
Cruella Just remember, you two! Dinner with me tomorrow night.

Mrs Dearly and Cruella exit. Mr Dearly and Nanny Butler enter

Mr Dearly (*elated*) Pongo, where are you? Here, boy. Missis is all right. Cook has rung for the Really Splendid Vet and he is on his way. But she's done very well. You'll never guess how many puppies you've got.
Pongo War?
Mr Dearly Four? No, more than that.
Pongo Weven?
Mr Dearly Seven? No, more.
Pongo Wen?

Nanny Butler Pongo! Sit! Just tell him, sir. If he understands at all, which I doubt very much indeed, you can at least tell him quickly.
Mr Dearly You're right, Butler of course. Pongo, you are the proud father of no less than fifteen beautiful puppies.
Pongo Wifteen? Wuffunderful! (*He swoons*)

The doorbell rings. Pongo recovers

Mr Dearly That will be the vet, Butler. Would you please?
Nanny Butler Of course.

Nanny Butler exits

Mr Dearly And now, Pongo, I know that father dogs are not supposed to be welcome when puppies have just been born, but you are very special.
Pongo Wuff! Wuff!
Mr Dearly So now we'll go straight to the broom cupboard and you can tell them all how happy you feel. Come on, Pongo.

Pongo and Mr Dearly exit

Pongo (*as they go*) Wuffteen wuppies! Wuffunderful!

The Lights fade on the dining-room. When ready, the Lights come up on the broom cupboard

Missis is reclining happily, surrounded by fifteen tiny puppies. Pongo is inspecting her and them extremely proudly

Pongo Is there anything troubling you, Missis? Anything at all. After all, fifteen is a rather large number. For the first time, I mean.
Missis Yes, there is something, Pongo.
Pongo Just tell me, my dear.
Missis Names.
Pongo (*mystified*) Names?
Missis I can't think of enough names for them all.
Pongo Oh, names! Well, I can see that could be a problem. Ouch! Well, I think we should call this one "Lucky". He just nipped me, and he's very lucky I didn't nip him back.
Missis This little one is really bossy.
Pongo She's very pretty.
Missis She has very bad manners. I think we should call her Cadpig.
Pongo Whatever you say, Missis. Now what about these two?

The Lights cross-fade to Regent's Park, London. Late afternoon, early evening

Some Denizens are walking their dogs; Mr and Mrs Dearly are walking purposefully towards the de Vil house into which they disappear

The weather is ominous, and indicating a thunderstorm which develops during and breaks out at the end of Scene 2

SCENE 2

Cruella de Vil's dining-room

A room with black marble walls and a white marble table. The room is decorated liberally with fur. A major feature of the laid table is a large pepper-pot which is used liberally at each course by Cruella

A Persian Cat sharpens its claws on the table, inspects the room, then hears a sound and hides

Cruella de Vil enters, followed by the Dearlys and James-Or-Whoever who helps the Dearlys remove their outer clothes, and then withdraws

Cruella Come in, come in, my darlings, do. The weather looks frightful. It's good and warm here in the dining-room, though. What do you think of it?

Mrs Dearly It's, well, it's very — very ...

Mr Dearly "Fitting" is the word you are looking for, my dear. The room is very fitting, Mrs de Vil.

Cruella Oh, haven't I told you? Call me Cruella. All my best friends' husbands do. "Fitting" — is that the in word? Most kind. I will remember it.

Mrs Dearly (*discovering the Persian Cat*) Is this your dear cat?

She makes as if to stroke it, a gesture the Persian Cat welcomes

Cruella Don't do that! I never do. It just encourages them. Get out of here, Cat! Cats, pets, children, they're all the same. They should never be seen in a dining-room. A dining-room is for dinner.

The Persian Cat exits most reluctantly, but obediently

Cruella sounds a gong then ushers the Dearlys to their seats

Servants enter carrying tureens, led by James-Or-Whoever

Cruella Dinner, James or whatever your name is. Dear friends, I hope you enjoy the first course.

Servant 1 serves the soup under James' supervision

Mrs Dearly It's an amazing house. Not so much the house itself, which is so like our own, but what you have done with it. And all those furs. I don't think I've seen as much fur in my life.

Cruella One simply has to keep warm. And the fur-business is how my husband makes our living.

Mr Dearly To judge by the décor, he obviously has a lot of home-work! Are we to meet him tonight?

Cruella People come to us from all over the world to buy their furs. We try to entertain here, but, we are constantly having to take them down to our farms. That's why he is missing this delightful dinner. But the soup will be getting cold. Do indulge, darlings.

Mrs Dearly What an unusual colour.

Cruella Do you think so? What soup is this, James-Or-Whoever?

James It is as you ordered, madam. Turtle soup.

Cruella What, purple turtle soup?

James You told the new cook purple was one of your favourite colours, madam.

Mrs Dearly has started to gag on the soup

Cruella And so it is. Where's the pepper?

Mr Dearly (*gagging and spluttering*) In the soup.

Cruella Is it not to your taste? James-Or-Whoever, serve the fish-dish.

Servant 2 serves the fish. It is bright green

Mr Dearly You mentioned that you had farms. Do fur-farms really exist?

Cruella Yes, my husband got the idea from Ford. Henry Ford. The American. Ford created a fortune out of making cars on production lines. So we thought, why not do the same with furs? We've got a baby seal farm in the Orkneys, a Persian lamb farm in the Cotswolds, and a farm somewhere in Suffolk where we're collecting D—— My dear, Mr Dearly, the fish will be missing you. Do feel free to sample.

Mrs Dearly Oh, please do, dear husband. You are so brave a sampler.

Cruella I must have my pepper. Now, where can it be? Ah, here it is.

Mr Dearly samples the fish and gags

How do you find it?

Mrs Dearly I think he finds it a touch hot.

Cruella How wonderful! Hot bream! Excellent with pepper.

James The fish is not bream, madam. The new cook thought you wanted green fish.

Cruella Is the new cook deaf or something?

James Madam is surely right.

Cruella James-Or-Whoever, serve the meat dish, at once.

Servant 3 lifts the lid of the meat dish to reveal a blue meat-joint and carvers

Mrs Dearly What an absolutely ... I don't think I've ever seen a blue joint of meat before.

James When the new cook asked madam how she liked her meat done, madam told her in no uncertain terms that she preferred it blue.

Cruella Did I? Well, well. And here it is, radiantly blue. Not at all what I intended. Remove it!

James hurries Servant 3 and the offending dish away

Staff these days are impossible. Now what was I saying?

Mr Dearly Getting back to all your fur-farms — is it a developing market?

Cruella Women will always want furs. How else does one keep warm? Apart from fires. And pepper, of course.

Mr Dearly You were explaining what you collected at your Suffolk farm.

Cruella Ah, was I, indeed? James-Or-Whoever, the dessert.

James beckons Servant 4

And then tell Cook to start packing her bag instantly. I will not have the wrong food being served at every course. Dessert, my darlings, will make up for everything. It is my special favourite.

Mr Dearly What could that be?

James Black ice-cream, madam. Sir.

Cruella Precisely. Black ice-cream liberally covered with the choicest black pepper.

Servant 4 accidentally, ruinously throws the dessert on to the table much to the relief of the Dearlys, the amusement of James and the other Servants and the wrath of Cruella who lets fly

You are sacked. All of you. Sacked, sacked, sacked, sacked. James-Or-Whoever, you will not leave until the last of my guests has departed.

The Servants burst into tears and exit

James Of course, madam.
Cruella And then you are sacked as well.

James bursts into tears and follows the weeping Servants out

As they leave, Cruella sees the Dearlys who have been horror-struck

My dears, take no notice. Servants are easily obtained. Children are so cheap and plentiful these days. Like animals.
Mr Dearly I'm afraid we must be going.
Cruella Already? It seems so very early.
Mr Dearly You reminded me we have responsibilities.
Cruella Did I? How careless of me.
Mrs Dearly Absolutely not, dear friend. It was most kind of you.
Cruella Kind? Of me? Why, what did I do?
Mr Dearly It was not so much what you did as what you said. You reminded us that we have to think of our Cook, our Butler and our animals. We must leave, Mrs Dearly. Good-night, and thank you.
Cruella It seems very sudden, but go if you must. James-Or-Whoever will be there to see to your coats and to your way home. But then you and those darling dogs are so close. It's been delightful.

The Dearlys exit

That was over sooner than I expected. Just as well. They are a tediously boring couple. But we need their dogs. Those fifteen little Dalmatians. To add to all the others. As de Vil says, fashion is the future — and he and I create fashion. We create the future. Indeed, we do. We are the future. I must carry on planning. Now I have got rid of the Cook, James-Or-Whoever, and those infantile servants, I must get the Badduns here from Suffolk. We need Saul and Jasper Baddun. Most of all we need their van. It's small and it's black. It's just about big enough and it won't be recognized in London. Yes, it is time for the Badduns.

Thunderstorm

The Lights cross-fade to Regent's Park, London. Late evening

Some denizens are walking their dogs; Mr and Mrs Dearly are walking purposefully towards their house into which they disappear. Servants and James pass by in a line carrying their suitcases

SCENE 3

The Dearlys' dining-room. The next morning

It is a gloomy day and raining outside

Nanny Cook and Nanny Butler enter followed by Pongo

Nanny Cook I don't like doing it. It's not really my job, you know.
Nanny Butler I am well aware of that, Cook, but at times like this we all have to give a hand. You take this end and I'll take the other.

They start clearing the table of a tablecloth. As they fold it, Pongo participates

Nanny Cook And what are we going to do about breakfast, anyway?
Nanny Butler Don't worry about it at all. Mrs Dearly's out looking for a foster-mother for the puppies and Mr Dearly's busy ——
Nanny Cook *A foster-mother?* Not another dog. We've already got seventeen. What on earth do we want another one for?
Nanny Butler Because the Splendid Vet said that Missis Pongo would get very tired and thin trying to feed fifteen puppies on her own. And if we weren't careful the strong puppies would get more milk than the weak ones.
Nanny Cook What's wrong with feeding them from bottles?
Nanny Butler Do you want to try and feed fifteen puppies with bottles? And do all the washing up afterwards?
Nanny Cook I suppose not. But why is Mrs Dearly doing the Searching?
Nanny Butler The Splendid Vet tried to, but couldn't find anyone. Mr Dearly's been up all night and is very, very tired. There's been another Government crisis — to do with money, of course. Mrs Dearly rang up some Lost Dogs' Homes and found a foster-mother who hadn't been claimed. So she's had to go out.
Nanny Cook Mrs Dearly should be back soon, though, and then we can get things back to normal.
Nanny Butler She should have been home half an hour ago — but it has been raining a lot, that will have slowed her down.

Hoot from a car from outside

Mrs Dearly (*off*) Nanny! *Nanny!*

Pongo barks

Nanny Cook That sounds like her now. She might need some help.
Nanny Butler You go and see. I'll go and wake Mr Dearly.

Nanny Butler exits

Nanny Cook goes towards the cry for help

Mrs Dearly enters, wearing outdoor clothes, rumpled, dishevelled and wet

Mrs Dearly I need some help, Nanny Cook. That was why I hooted with the
car. Where is Mr Dearly?
Nanny Cook Mr Dearly? Mr Dearly is still asleep after being up all night
trying to help Missis feed her babies with those bottles we made. Nanny
Butler's gone to wake him up. Now what do you need help with, my dear?
Mrs Dearly I need help with what I've got in the car. Help to get it out and
into the house safely. We will need some shampoo, a flannel and water, that
would be best.
Nanny Cook What will we need?
Mrs Dearly Shampoo! Flannel! Water!

Mr Dearly enters, sleepily, not seeing his wife

Nanny Cook Right-ho.
Mr Dearly What is it? What is it Nanny Cook?
Nanny Cook Mrs Dearly has come back, sir. She must have got very dirty.
She wants a shampoo, a flannel, and some water.

Pongo mouths the items

Mr Dearly Hallo, my dear. Back early? Very dirty, eh? That sounds like bad
news.
Mrs Dearly Not really. Nanny Cook could you go and get the things I
mentioned. Shampoo, flannel and water.

Pongo repeats the items

And ask Nanny Butler to help you empty the car.

Nanny Cook exits

It's good news.

Mr Dearly You have found the foster-mother.

Mrs Dearly Yes, dear. I have named her Perdita.

Mr Dearly Is she from the Dog's Home?

Mrs Dearly No, she isn't. When I got there, the dog I'd gone to see had been claimed by her owners. So I started to come straight back.

Mr Dearly And it was raining.

Mrs Dearly Yes, it was. Dark, gloomy and wet. I must look frightful.

Mr Dearly Please go on, dear.

Mrs Dearly Well I was staring hard through the windscreen wipers trying to see where to go, when I saw what looked like a bundle lying in the road. I thought something had been run over. So I stopped the car and got out.

Mr Dearly And that's why you're so wet.

Mrs Dearly I saw it was a dog, and I thought it was dead. But then it sort of woke up and tried to get to its feet. I couldn't leave it there, and it looked so hungry, so I picked it up and carried it to the car. It was like a sack of bones. And so dirty! Then when I got to the car, I saw in the car lights that it was a mother dog with some milk to give.

Mr Dearly So you brought her straight home.

Mrs Dearly Of course not. I took her to the Splendid Vet. He checked her over, and said she needed some good food and was otherwise fine. And he said it looked as though her own puppies had been taken away and she was looking for them. She'll make a fine foster-mother.

Mr Dearly Did he say anything else?

Mrs Dearly He said she ought to have a bath or she might give the puppies fleas.

Nanny Cook enters excitedly

Nanny Cook Guess what! Guess what!

Mr Dearly
Mrs Dearly } (*together*) What?
Pongo

Nanny Cook I've washed the foster-mother and guess what!

Mrs Dearly She's very thin and needs a good dinner or two.

Nanny Cook Yes, that's obvious. But guess what!

Mr Dearly She's covered in fleas? She has no milk to give?

Nanny Cook Yes, that's obvious. But guess what!

Pongo Wuff, wuff, wuffitt? Woff, woof?

Nanny Cook That's obvious, too, Pongo. But guess what! What wasn't obvious until we'd washed her clean was that she's a sort of Dalmatian.

Mr Dearly
Mrs Dearly } (*together, surprised*) Ohhh!
Pongo

Nanny Cook But instead of black spots, she's got liver-coloured spots.
Mr Dearly ⎫
Mrs Dearly ⎬ (*together, pleasantly surprised*) Ohhh!
Pongo ⎭
Mr Dearly Then she is very unusual and very valuable. That is excellent news, eh Pongo?
Pongo Wuff!
Mr Dearly We must introduce her to Missis and the puppies.
Mrs Dearly No, dear. The Splendid Vet said that first we must introduce her to Pongo. Perhaps you can do that. I must get out of these wet things.

Mrs Dearly exits

Nanny Cook And I have to get lunch ready. We must all be very hungry. Especially Perdita.
Mr Dearly And I need some sleep. (*Yawning*) Feeding these puppies is exhausting. But now we have the foster-mother. It's all right, Pongo, I'll let her in to see you. I'll leave you two together.

Mr Dearly exits

A pause

Perdita enters cautiously. She freezes as she sees Pongo

Pongo circles Perdita

Pongo Hallo. The pets named me Pongo. I am most grateful you are here. My lady has been named Missis and she will be most grateful too.
Perdita I was called Spot. Your female pet called me Perdita.
Pongo Perdita. From Shakespeare.
Perdita No. I came originally from Epping, actually.
Pongo You misunderstand me. The name, Perdita, comes from a book written by a human called Shakespeare.
Perdita I see. How do you know?
Pongo I was very hungry once and devoured his Complete Works.
Perdita Were they very filling?
Pongo They were extremely satisfying. The name Perdita means she who is lost, I think. So you must have a story to tell. Where were you born?
Perdita I was born in a large country house near Epping and the forest. I had a slightly curly tail, so I was given to a farmer. He wasn't very fond of me, so he let me run wild a bit.
Pongo And that's not good for any of us dogs.

Perdita When I wanted to marry, the farmer didn't arrange anything and no dog ever came a-courting.

Pongo So, of course, you went to find one for yourself.

Perdita And I did! I did! He was superb, valuably dressed, a really magnificent collar, and it was love at first sight. He had a strange marking that made him different from any dog I've ever seen.

Pongo What marking was that?

Perdita A mark like the shape of a dumb-bell. A dumb-bell on his nose. Do you know what I mean?

Pongo Yes, I do. A Dalmatian with a dumb-bell marking on his nose. They are very, very rare. So, what happened?

Perdita We rushed off into the woods to arrange things, married, and promised to love each other for always. Then he took me back out of the woods and the awful thing happened.

Pongo What was that?

Perdita My farmer came along in his rattling old car and grabbed me and took me home.

Pongo Did you struggle? Did you howl?

Perdita We both did. But the pets paid no attention to us at all.

Pongo What a sad, sad story.

Perdita There's more. Nine weeks after we were married, I had eight puppies. The farmer did not feed me more or help me in any way, so I got thinner and thinner. You can see.

Pongo And what about the puppies?

Perdita The farmer fed them. But never enough, so they kept on wanting my milk. And I got thinner still. But the puppies got more and more beautiful. Well, that's what a human visitor called them. Beautiful, she said.

Pongo Well, that was good.

Perdita Until that dreadful afternoon. I woke up to find there wasn't one puppy in the farmhouse, in the farmyard or anywhere on the farm. I looked everywhere. I ran right down to the road, in case they'd been run over.

Pongo You barked, of course.

Perdita I went on and on, barking every now and again. Nothing. Then it began to rain and a car nearly hit me. So I jumped into a muddy ditch. I crawled out and walked on, still barking until I collapsed in the road. And then your human found me and brought me here.

Pongo And here you will get good food, and see some lovely puppies. And I am sure yours are not lost at all. Beautiful puppies are most likely to have been sold — and that could be the best thing of all. What would your farmer have done with nine dogs?

Perdita That's true, I suppose. He would never have fed them properly. And he might have drowned them or shot them or something. But I miss them so.

Pongo First mothers always do. And now, I think it's best if we go and get some sleep. You are most welcome here. You will need rest, water and food to be absolutely ready for my little ones. Follow me.

Pongo and Perdita exit

<h2 style="text-align:center">Scene 4</h2>

The Dearlys' dining-room. Some weeks later. Afternoon

Pongo enters, followed by Lucky and three other puppies, Cadpig, Patch, and Roly-Poly

Missis enters

Cadpig explores the room curiously. Missis teaches Lucky and Patch how to wash. Pongo plays Catch and Chase with Lucky

Mr Dearly (*off*) Pongo! Missis! Perdita! Walk-time. Walk-time.

Pongo and Missis exit barking

The Puppies play chase with each other and chew the furniture

Nanny Cook enters with a broom

Nanny Cook I keep on telling them, it's not my job. It's not my job at all. But do they listen? Of course not. Every afternoon's the same — off they go, taking the three big dogs for a walk — or is it the dogs taking them for a walk, I never really know. So they leave me with all the work to do, tea to get, and fifteen puppies to look after. Puppies — huh, they're nearly dogs by now. They are everywhere.

The sound of a strident car-horn

Up to all kinds of mischief — real scamps.

Doorbell rings

And now the doorbell. It would be wouldn't it.

Nanny Cook scoots the dogs away, and exits with all, except one

The one hides

Nanny Cook returns without the broom, followed by Cruella de Vil who is wearing the white mink cloak, and beneath it a brown mink coat, a fur hat, fur-lined boots and fur gloves

Nanny Cook And I'm afraid the master, the mistress and Butler are all out, Miss.

Cruella What dreadfully bad timing. I'll just stay here and wait then. Carry on working—but before you start, do tell me about the puppies. I saw them as I came in. Such pretty markings. They'll be about ready to leave their mother, I suppose?

Nanny Cook Very nearly, Miss. But they won't have to.

Cruella Indeed? Tell me, why not, pray?

Nanny Cook Because Mr and Mrs Dearly have told us all loud and often that they are going to keep them. All of them.

Cruella How nice.

Nanny Cook As you're determined on staying here, Miss, can I take your cloak and your hat or something?

Cruella Certainly not. I'll need them. I mean, it's kind of you to ask, but I need to keep warm at all times. And it's freezing outside. Where are you going?

Nanny Cook To look out the window and see if the master and mistress are coming back yet. Oh, that's strange.

Cruella What is?

Nanny Cook That small black van standing opposite the house.

Cruella Oh, I saw it as I came in. Just a delivery van, I expect. Ouch!

Nanny Cook (*going to her*) What's the matter, Miss? (*She attends to Cruella*)

Jasper Baddun creeps in stealthily and dog-naps the hidden puppy

Cruella Something bit me or stung me or something. What could have done that? It can't be a wasp or a bee, it's the wrong time of year. Perhaps it was dog lice. How horrid. Absolutely horrid.

Nanny Cook Can't be dog lice, Miss. All the dogs is bathed regular, and shampooed proper, just like the vet says.

Cruella Well, I felt something bite. Have a look around, do. Is it under the table?

Nanny Cook Nothing there, Miss. I'll check the window. Oooh, well I never ——

Cruella You found something?

Nanny Cook No, Miss. But that black van just drove off at a terrific speed.

The sound of Cruella's car-horn, twice

Cruella Well, I must away. I've been here far too long. Don't worry about this bite, I'll sort it out at home. Don't mention my visit to the Dearlys. I'll drop back round later, after tea, and tell them myself.
Nanny Cook This way, Miss.
Cruella I'll see myself out. That's perfectly all right.

Cruella exits

Nanny Cook Well, thank goodness she's gone. I don't like that woman and all her furs. And talking of furs, I'd better get those little puppies in. They've only got their thin little skins — in this weather they'll catch their death of cold.

Nanny Cook exits

A pause

Mr Dearly (*off*) Now get inside in the warm, you dogs, while we get our coats off.

Pongo and Missis enter

Pongo Well, that was the briskest of walks. Utterly invigorating and refreshing. You looked wonderful in your new blue coat. Did you enjoy yourself, my dear?
Missis Yes, I did — most of the time.
Pongo Most of the time? Why not all of the time?
Missis Because at the very end when we came into the house I thought I caught the smell of that dreadful human. That Cruella de Vil human.
Pongo Oh, I don't think so. I didn't catch her odour.
Missis You were too busy thinking how nice it is taking pets for a walk, I expect.
Pongo Well, it does do them a lot of good. Fresh air, a bit of stick throwing, and they are so good when they're on the lead. None of that bobbing and weaving about they do when they're off the lead. No, I'm sure a walk is really good for them.

Mr Dearly enters, followed by Mrs Dearly

Mr Dearly Well, I hope you enjoyed that, you two ——
Pongo Wuff. Wuffimuch.

Mr Dearly Where's Perdita?

Mrs Dearly I sent her down to get the puppies in. They've been out far too long. And I sent Nanny Butler to buy some more food — for the dogs.

From off, a scream from Nanny Cook and panic-stricken barking from Perdita

Perdita (*off*) Wuppies!

Mr Dearly What on earth is that?

Pongo Wuppies?

Missis What?

Mrs Dearly It sounded like Cook — screaming. You must find out what's wrong.

Mr Dearly heads for the door

> *The door is flung open by the distraught and tearful Nanny Cook who enters, followed by a barking Perdita. There is pandemonium with pets and dogs running everywhere*

Mr Dearly (*stopping them*) Now, will you all calm down. Right now. Nanny Cook, will you please explain what is wrong, and why you are in tears.

Nanny Cook Gone. Gone. They've gone!

The pandemominum restarts

Mr Dearly (*stopping them*) Who has gone? We are all here!

Nanny Cook The puppies. All gone. Stolen!

> *Pongo, Perdita and Missis howl and exit barking to search the house*

Mrs Dearly How do you know they were stolen?

Nanny Cook Saw a black van driving away. I thought it was strange. I told her. What do we do?

Mr Dearly What can we do?

Mrs Dearly Dearly, go over there and ring the police. Your friend at Scotland Yard.

Mr Dearly That's a good idea. (*He does so*)

Mrs Dearly You go and check outside, Cook. See if you can find anything, anything at all.

Nanny Cook Anything that's tall.

Nanny Cook exits

We hear the dogs barking round the house

Mrs Dearly And I'll go and sort those dogs out! Missis! Perdita! Pongo!

Mrs Dearly exits

Mr Dearly remains oblivious, telephoning

Pongo and Missis enter from different directions

Missis Any news?

Pongo Cook has found a piece of sacking on the wall.

Missis So they were put into sacks and taken away.

Pongo In a black van. Why are you sniffing?

Missis I can smell that human. That Cruella de Vil's been here. I bet she had something to do with it.

Pongo You're obsessed. I can't smell her at all. She's not been here. Anyway, she doesn't drive a black van.

Missis That's true. And Butler or Cook would have said so. So our puppies were put into sacks. Think of little baby Cadpig in the dark in a sack. (*She sobs*) She'll be so frightened.

Pongo Big brother Patch will take care of her. And little Lucky, too, he's so brave he'll bite anyone who tries to harm her.

Missis And then the thieves will kill him.

Pongo No-one will kill anyone. Our puppies were stolen because they are so valuable. But they are only valuable while they are alive.

Missis What are the humans doing?

Pongo What did you say? The humans? Mr Dearly's ringing the police; Cook's wringing her hands; Mrs Dearly's standing with Perdita; and Butler's back home standing with Cook.

Missis Well, that won't do much good, will it. What time is it?

Pongo looks out of the window

Pongo It's getting dark. It must be nearly twilight. (*Realizing*) Oh, you clever Missis Pongo. I hadn't thought of that. Twilight Barking. Of course.

Missis Yes, Twilight Barking. What message will you send?

Pongo Let me see now. I must start with " Help. Help. Help."

Missis The Emergency Call. Good.

Pongo Then I'll say: "Fifteen Dalmatian puppies missing".

Missis Say "stolen" — that's more urgent.

Pongo "Fifteen Dalmatian puppies stolen. Send news to Pongo and Missis Pongo, of Regent's Park, London. End of message." That should do something.

Missis Well, let's go and send the message straight away.

Pongo and Missis exit. Mrs Dearly enters

Mrs Dearly So what exactly did your friend at Scotland Yard tell you?

Mr Dearly He promised to do what he could. But he warned me that stolen dogs are seldom recovered unless a reward is offered. In our case a big reward.

Mrs Dearly So what have you done about it?

Mr Dearly I have rung up the newspapers and put some big advertisements in tonight's papers and in tomorrow morning's papers.

Mrs Dearly Well, that should do something. I suppose we ought to sit by the telephone tonight and wait for people to ring. Where are Pongo and Missis Pongo?

Mr Dearly Outside, I think. I saw them heading for the back.

Pongo and Missis are seen outside. We hear three short, sharp loud barks from Pongo

Missis Again, Pongo. Help! Help! Help!

Pongo Wuff! Wuff! Wuff!

Missis "Fifteen Dalmatian puppies stolen. Send news to Pongo and Missis Pongo, of Regent's Park, London. End of message."

Pongo "Wuffwuff wuff-wuff'n wuff-wuff wuff-wuff. Wuff wuff wuff wuff-wuff wuff wuff-wuff wuff-wuff wuff wuff-wuff wuff wuff wuff. Wuff wuff. Wuffo."

Mrs Dearly We must get them in. I know dogs like to bark in the early evening, but I wish sometimes ...

The bark-message is repeated

Mr Dearly It's almost as though they're sending a message. Just listen!

We hear the bark-message being repeated in the distance by a different dog

Mrs Dearly Sometimes, I get very worried about you. Dogs can't talk, so how could they ever send messages? We must go downstairs and sort out telephone duties with Cook and Butler.

Mr and Mrs Dearly exit

As they go, we hear a deeper, distant, quite lengthy bark-message from a third dog

Missis I didn't understand that last Barking Message completely.

Pongo It came from one who said he was a Great Dane. He said he was near Hampstead Heath. He lives outside while his humans live inside. He has a chain of friends all over England and will stay on duty day and night.

Missis A Great Dane, eh? That's very encouraging. They are true gentle-dogs. And aren't they related to us? Watch out: humans!

Pongo You go with them. Try and find out what they are doing. I'll stay outside and listen for any replies.

Missis exits. Pongo continues to bark, as he leaves

The Dearlys, Nanny Cook and Perdita enter, followed by Missis

Missis and Perdita go into conference. A lengthy Barking Message is heard faintly in the background from Pongo, off

Mr Dearly So, Cook, if you would take the first watch, that would be an immense help. I don't think a great deal will happen before the morning papers come out. But you never know.

Nanny Cook But what about dinner?

Mrs Dearly Now don't you worry yourself about that, my dear. Butler and I will take care of dinner. Just you make sure you take all the messages. I'll go and see Butler right now. Come, dear!

The Dearlys exit

As Nanny Cook goes to sit down, the telephone rings

Nanny Cook Hallo. This is 5065. ... Scotland Yard. You are from *Scotland Yard*! ... You'd like to speak with Mr Dearly! Our Mr Dearly. ... Yes, indeed, you have got the right number. I'll go and get him to the telephone immediately.

Nanny Cook exits at speed. Pongo enters at speed

Pongo Did you hear the message from the Great Dane?

Missis I tried to, but the humans kept on talking.

Pongo I sent the message in every direction — and kept on hearing " No news. Deepest regrets. End of message". Until there was only the Great Dane left. And he began to send "Deepest regrets" and then suddenly sent "Wait! Wait! Wait!"

Perdita And then? And then?

Pongo And then he sent the message "News! News at last. Stand by to receive details."

Missis What were the details?

Pongo The Great Dane got them from a Pomeranian who heard them from a Poodle who heard them from a Boxer who heard them from a Pekinese who ——

Perdita We don't really care about who — we care about what.

Pongo But some 480 dogs have relayed messages over 60 miles as the dog barks. And every single one has made it an "Urgent" message.

Missis But what is the message?

Pongo It came from a sheepdog in Suffolk. He and a tabby cat found an old, dry bone outside a house with huge walls. The house is looked after by two horrible humans, Saul and Jasper.

Perdita So what's so special about an old dry bone?

Pongo This one was special because it had SOS scratched on it. SOS means Save Our Skins. And when the cat climbed a tree to look over the wall, she saw the house and its gardens were seething with them.

Missis Seething with what, Pongo?

Pongo Why, seething with Dalmatian puppies. And I've got instructions for getting there, too.

Missis So we must leave tonight to rescue them.

Perdita All of us?

Pongo No, you must stay behind. In case of messages.

Missis Yes, Perdita. You must stay. You're better at barking than me. We must leave at once.

Pongo Not before we've had dinner. It's a long way to Suffolk and it may be a long time before we get another meal.

Perdita Watch out — human on the way. If we could only get them to understand us.

Pongo Then they could drive us to Suffolk in their car.

Perdita Sixty miles is a long way.

Pongo They could send their police.

Missis The humans are too busy with telephones, advertisements, newspapers, and Scotland Yard to listen to us. Even if they could understand us. Which they can't.

Perdita Humans don't listen.

Pongo They listen, but they do not understand. You are both right. So we must go out into the country and find the puppies on our own.

Perdita Out into the country? On your own? That could be very dangerous. You two are town dogs, not country dogs. Let me go.

Missis You are right, dear, absolutely right. But what is more important — danger to us or danger to our puppies?

Pongo Perdita, you must stay here for messages. Receiving and sending, please. Come on, Missis, we as parents must lose no more time. We must leave for the country at once.

They do, pawing farewell to Perdita

CURTAIN

ACT II

SCENE 1

The road to Suffolk. Daytime

Woodland

Pongo and Missis enter

Pongo You are shivering, Missis. Are you cold?

Missis No, Pongo. (*She continues to shiver*)

Pongo Well, I am. I think you and I have become a bit pampered. We must not lose our liking for adventure; we must never forget our wild ancestry.

Missis No, Pongo. I just wish I'd brought my lovely, new blue coat.

Pongo The more we worry about our missing puppies, the less we will be able to help them. We must think clearly. We must be brave, we must know we cannot fail to find them. If we think positively, nothing can stop us. Are you warmer now, Missis?

Missis Yes, Pongo. (*She shivers and her tail droops*)

Pongo Watch out! Human on the way!

They hide

The figure of a uniformed Policeman passes, searching

Pongo and Missis come out from hiding

Missis Pongo, that policeman reminded me. We are illegal. We are out without our collars. (*She shivers*)

Pongo I know that. I thought it was a good idea. Humans can grab us by our collars. So, no collars. But I wish we'd brought your new blue coat.

Missis Where do you think we are?

Pongo I think we are north-east of London and in a forest. I remember hearing that there is a very old forest called Epping around this way. Perdita told me about it.

Missis Has this Epping Forest got any rivers, do you think? I am very thirsty.

Pongo I can smell smoke. There must be a village nearby.

Missis And where there's a village, there's bound to be ——

A bark off

A Golden Retriever enters

Pongo ⎫ (*together*) — a Golden Retriever.
Missis ⎭

Retriever Pongo and Missis Pongo, I presume. We heard you were coming this way. The Dawn Barking told us. Is there anything you need?

Pongo Nothing, thank you ——

Missis Yes, there is. Could you possibly find us some water?

Retriever Water! Yes, naturally. There's a stream close by. It's fresh and clean. And one of our best beds lies quite near.

Missis A bed? At this time of day?

Retriever We thought you would probably prefer to sleep by day and travel by night. Less chance of being caught, doncha know.

Pongo Caught? Who would want to catch us?

Retriever The police. Who else? Your pets believe you've been taken by the same humans that stole your puppies. So they've told the police. And the police are out looking for you.

Pongo We should sleep by day and travel by night. Good idea.

Missis So, where could we spend the daytime?

Retriever As I said, in one of our best bedrooms. A safe, secure day of rest. Follow me.

The Retriever leads Pongo and Missis to what looks like a broken-down stagecoach

I could take you back to the inn that I run with my humans. But it wouldn't be wise.

Pongo No indeed. We might be discovered.

Retriever So I decided this retired coach would be a better hiding-place.

Pongo A far more appropriate place — after all, our ancestors were trained to run behind coaches and carriages.

Missis Some people still call us Coach Dogs or Carriage Dogs. (*She starts to explore*)

Retriever And your run from London has shown you are truly worthy of your ancestors. This coach will be quite safe. Now, do tell me: what's it really like to live in London? It must be so exciting!

Missis Pongo! There's a beautiful bed of straw; two lovely chops to eat; what looks like iced cakes and a box of chocolates!

Retriever They've come from the dog-butcher; the dog-baker and the dog-confectioner in the village. We all want you to feel well cared for in your important mission.

Pongo How can we ever thank you?
Retriever By finding your puppies and taking them safely home. Do have
a pleasant sleep. Good-morning!

The Retriever exits

Pongo Good-morning to you.
Missis Good-morning, Retriever. Now, Pongo, first sleep, then food.

Pongo and Missis go to settle down

Missis Watch out! Human! A small human.
Pongo I smell no real danger. So we won't hide.

A Child enters

Child Here doggy, doggy. Come here. I've got something for you. It's all
right, don't be afraid. I won't hurt you.

*Pongo gets within a couple of yards. The Child throws a stone which hits
Pongo and hurts him. Pongo goes for the child, but Missis restrains him*

The Child scampers off, laughing

Man (*off*) Where are you? Oh, there you are. Now what have you been
doing? Dogs? What kind of dogs? Where? We haven't got time for that.

Pongo and Missis back down

Missis Are you hurt, Pongo? (*She inspects him*) There's nothing a good rest
won't cure.
Pongo We can't stay here and rest. The child will tell the human what and
where we are. And the human will tell the police ... We must move on.
Missis But where can we go to next?
Pongo Head north and east. We are looking for a town called Sudbury. It said
so in the Barking.
Missis Is that where our puppies are?
Pongo Nearly. But first we have to get to Sudbury.
Spaniel (*off*) That's not far from the house of my human. Why do you want
to go to Sudbury?
Pongo (*bristling*) Who's there? Come out and show yourself!
Missis Calm down, Pongo. It's a dog, I'm sure.
Pongo Can't be too careful. There are such things as bad dogs, remember.

A Spaniel enters

Spaniel Good-day. Can I be of any help to you? If you really want to get to Sudbury, my human's carriage is just down the road. His gardener and I have been collecting hornbeam shoots for my pet. Jump aboard, and we'll take you to Sudbury.

Pongo Come on, Missis. I don't suppose you have water or food on the carriage, do you?

Spaniel Of course, we do. But you must tell me what you are doing here. And why you want to go to Sudbury.

Pongo Don't you listen to the Barkings? The Twilight, the Midnight or the Dawn Barkings, I mean.

Spaniel Haven't listened to them for years. I live too far away, really. Besides, reception is very bad nowadays. Now do tell me why you want to go to Sudbury.

Pongo, limping, exits, followed by Missis and the Spaniel who are chattering

There is the sound of a car driving off. Then the sound of another vehicle arriving

The Baddun Brothers, Saul and Jasper, enter on a lightweight motor-cycle. They search around

Saul Well, there's nothing here, Jasper.

Jasper And I've found nothing, Saul.

Saul So either those two big Dalmatian dogs have gone on ahead, or that kid and his father were telling lies.

Jasper Let's go back and wallop them. Especially that kid. I didn't like him at all.

Saul Nor did I. I thought he was going to chuck a stone at me. Little tyke. But the dad was a bit big for walloping, even for two of us. No, we must get on home. We have to make sure we're on guard in case those Dalmatians do try and rescue their horrible little puppies.

Jasper Well if they do try, and we catch them, it'll be two more skins for the Boss-lady. So she'll be pleased.

Saul And there's not a lot pleases her. Come on now, back to Hell Hall. Right?

Jasper
Saul } (*together*) Right!

Jaspet And I can watch the television. It's our favourite programme tonight.

Saul Not ...? Not *What's My Crime?*

Jasper Yeah! Yippee!

The Badduns drive off

Scene 2

The interior of Sudbury Manor. Afternoon to evening

Missis, Pongo and the Spaniel enter

Spaniel Now, Missis, Pongo. Welcome to Sudbury Manor. Tea will be served any time now.

A pair of double-doors opens to reveal Sir Charles seated in a chair beside a large fire

Beside the chair is a table laid for tea: a silver kettle boiling above a spirit lamp; silver cover protecting a plate with a number of slices of bread; butter dish; a cake dish; cup; saucer; silver bowl; milk jug; knife; toasting fork

Tea-time. I told you. Now go and hide behind the chair.

Pongo and Missis do as they are told

Sir Charles Wagging your tail, are you? Hungry, eh? Well, we've a good fire for our toast. (*He places a slice of bread on an extremely long toasting fork*) This won't take long. Just the one side you prefer, yes? And here you are.

Sir Charles throws the toast to the Spaniel who demolishes it, as Sir Charles watches

Good, boy. Hungry, eh?
Missis He's not very polite, is he? What about offering me — us — a piece.
Pongo Give him a chance, Missis.

The same procedure happens again, except that having given the Spaniel the toast, Sir Charles turns away. The Spaniel flicks the toast across to Pongo and Missis. This new turn of events happens several times, with the Spaniel only eating when Sir Charles is looking. Finally all the bread is gone

Sir Charles Well, that's the toast for today. Now how about some tea?

He offers the Spaniel the silver bowl. The Spaniel accepts, makes to drink from it, but as Sir Charles turns away, Pongo and Missis slurp it up gratefully. This happens several times

    (*Pleased*) Never known you with such a good appetite, my boy. (*He yawns*) Well, that's the tea for today. Time for a post-prandial forty winks, if you'll excuse me. (*He seems to settle down and go to sleep*)

Missis How wonderful! Hot buttered toast and sweet, milky tea. I'll remember that for ever.

Pongo We ought to be on our way.

Missis I feel so sleepy after that lovely tea.

Sir Charles starts in his sleep, wakes up and sees Pongo and Missis

Sir Charles Well, if that isn't Pongo and his Missis. What a pleasure! What a pleasure!

Spaniel (*whispering*) Don't move! Either of you!

Sir Charles Can you see them? If you can, don't be frightened. They must have died some fifty years before you were born.

Spaniel He thinks you are ghosts.

Pongo How does he know our names?

Sir Charles Pongo and his Missis, that's what we always called Dalmatians. They were the first dogs I ever knew. They used to run behind our carriages, but in the end they became just house dogs. They used to sit just there in front of the fire. Well, what a joy to know that dogs go on, too — I always hoped it was so. I shan't be long myself now, dogs, so just remember. (*He nods off to sleep*)

Spaniel You have given my human a great deal of pleasure. I am deeply grateful. We must look after our pets, you know.

Pongo What a lovely old gentleman. Now we must get back to our task. We need to go further on into Suffolk and find a folly.

Spaniel Yes, you told me in the carriage.

Missis What's a folly?

Pongo It's something the humans build that has no real use.

Missis How will we know we're at the right folly, then?

Spaniel Won't someone be there to meet you?

Pongo I expect so. Now how do you think we get there?

Missis The Twilight Barking will help us, I am sure.

Pongo and the Spaniel go into a huddle and discuss the route. We hear lots of "lefts" and "rights" at which Missis starts to look dazed. Pongo and the Spaniel laugh

Pongo We must say our goodbyes to you.

Spaniel Just come this way, and I'll make sure you have enough food for the journey.

Missis But how long do you think it will be before we see our puppies?

Pongo With good luck, we should reach them tomorrow morning. Isn't that so, Spaniel?

Spaniel With good luck, yes. Will you try to get me a message to say that you have them safe and sound?

Missis Of course we will.

Spaniel Now come this way, you two.

Pongo, Missis and the Spaniel exit

Sir Charles is still asleep. A pause. A thunderous knock at a front door. Protesting noises from outside

Saul and Jasper enter. Jasper approaches Sir Charles

A door slams, which wakes Sir Charles

Sir Charles What was that? Who are you?

Saul It's all right. We just want to ask you a few questions.

Jasper A few questions.

Sir Charles But who are you?

Saul That's irreverent.

Jasper Yeah, that's irreverent.

Saul Now, have you or have you not seen two Dalmatian dogs here today?

Jasper Yeah, big 'orrible white ones with black spots on. Like the pudding.

Sir Charles I know what Dalmatians look like. We used to keep them here as carriage dogs. Pongo and Missis.

Saul takes a piece of paper from his pocket and looks at it

Saul That's it. Pongo and Missis. That's wot their names was. Have you seen them today?

Sir Charles Yes, as a matter of fact I have.

Jasper Where, exackly?

Sir Charles Here, right here. In front of the fire.

Saul When, exackly?

Sir Charles At tea-time. Well, to be exact, just after tea.

Jasper And what was they doing, exackly?

Sir Charles Just sitting here, warming themselves at the fire. As they always did.

Jasper Warming themselves. At the fire.

Saul As they always did? What do ya mean by that?

Sir Charles Exactly what I said. As they always did, when they were alive.

Jasper When they were alive? But they are alive.

Sir Charles Oh, don't be ridiculous. They'd be over sixty human years old. No dog lives that long. None that I've heard of anyway. They were just ghosts.

Jasper G-g-g-ghosts? You've seen g-g-g-g-g-ghosts?

Sir Charles Of course I have. Haven't you? This house is full of ghosts.

Jasper He's bonkers. I'm off.

Saul Me too. What are we going to tell the Boss-lady?

Jasper You're in charge. That's your problem. I want to go home and watch my television.

Saul
Jasper } (*together*) Run for your life!

The Badduns exit at speed

Sir Charles What a strange pair. They seemed frightened or something. I was really glad to see those dogs after all these years.

SCENE 3

Outside Hell Hall. Night

It is cloudy moonlight. Lieutenant Cat, a tabby cat, is hidden in a tree

Pongo and Missis enter

Missis Are we nearly there, Pongo?

Pongo I don't know, Missis. We've passed the humans' folly. But we've missed Twilight Barking, so I couldn't send out any news. Nobody will be looking out for us.

Missis So we could have gone straight past wherever we are going without knowing.

Pongo Indeed we could have gone straight past. It is so dark. And there is nobody here.

Missis I can smell something.

Lieutenant Cat (*from the darkness*) Meeaow!

Missis A cat. Up there. In that tree.

Lieutenant Cat (*appearing*) Pongo? Missis? You are friendly, I presume?

Pongo Yes, indeed.

Lieutenant Cat Good. We've been expecting you. Now, you'll want food, drink and a good long rest.

Missis Could we see our puppies before we eat or sleep?

Pongo You won't find it easy to climb that tree, Missis.

Lieutenant Cat You won't need to. The Colonel has made other arrangements. And anyway the puppies won't be up until the Badduns let them out. Not for hours yet.

Missis The Badduns? Who are they?

Lieutenant Cat The Badduns are the ones that she-human put in charge of looking after the puppies.

Missis Who is "that she-human"?

Lieutenant Cat The lady of Hell Hall. Here comes the Colonel now.

Colonel Sheepdog enters

He's an absolute master of strategy — you just ask any of the sheep. He calls me his lieutenant. He's a proper officer. Best stand to attention. Like me.

They do. The darkness is lightening, revealing a great wall and iron gates

Colonel Morning. You must be the ones we are expecting. Now let's have a look at you. Straighten up, straighten up. Excellent, excellent. Glad to see you're large Dalmatians. Now what's been happening to you? There was a rare old fuss on Twilight Barking last night. No-one had any news, d'you see.

Missis We were being given a great deal of help by a spaniel at Sudbury.

Colonel Help, eh? Sudbury Spaniel? Sounds like a splendid fellow. Isn't he on the Barking?

Missis gestures towards her ears

What? Oh, bad reception, eh? Pity. Poor dog. Now, there's food and water over there for them that's hungry.

Missis What we'd like most is to get a glimpse of our puppies. After all, we have come a long way.

Lieutenant Cat Sir, I've told them the pups won't be out for hours yet.

Colonel Well done, Lieutenant. Now you two, I'd get some food inside me before I started worrying.

Pongo Worrying? Is there something wrong?

Colonel Private Pongo, I give you my word as your commanding officer, pro tem, that there is nothing wrong with your puppies.

Missis What did you call this place, Lieutenant?

Lieutenant Cat It's known as Hell Hall.

Colonel It used to be an ordinary farmhouse called Hill Hall. Then it stayed empty for about thirty years.

Lieutenant Cat Until she came. And painted the house black outside and red inside. She lets the Badduns live there free, as long as they look after things for her.

Missis But who is she?

Colonel She's the woman in charge. The lady of Hell Hall, we call her. One of our sheep platoons informs us she has been collecting Dalmatians from all over the country.

Pongo How many has she got in there?

Lieutenant Cat Almost a hundred, actually. Try counting them.

Missis Almost one hundred?

Pongo What in dogbasket would she want with so many Dalmatians?

Colonel It's the woman's idea, of course.

Missis Which woman?

Colonel The woman in charge. She's married to a furrier. I understand she only married him for his furs.

Missis We know of her! You must mean Cruella de Vil!

Lieutenant Cat That's her name. Devil.

Pongo And she's planning to set up a Dalmatian fur farm? To sell Dalmatian coats?

Colonel That's exactly what she wants to do.

Missis No Dalmatian will ever be safe until we stop that woman. And save our puppies!

Colonel Precisely!

Pongo The woman has to be stopped. There is no time left. She is always in a hurry. We have to get those dogs out of there. Not just our puppies. All of them. Now.

Colonel Don't panic you two. Plans now, action later. Remember that!

Pongo Plans now, action later, Missis. Plans now, action later.

Colonel Then let's go and make plans.

The Colonel, Missis and Pongo exit

SCENE 4

The kitchen of Hell Hall. Evening

The Badduns are watching television, by the light of a flickering fire. They are surrounded by the vaguely perceived shapes of dogs, including Lucky, Little Cadpig, Patch and Roly Poly. A dog barks

Jasper Which one of you was it? Stop it. You know the rules. No barking. Any of you. Shut it!

Saul Just come over here, Jasper, and shut up.

Another dog barks

Jasper Which one of you was it? If it barks again, it goes straight outside into the cold.

Saul All right, Jasper. Just sit down and watch the telly.

They do

The Colonel, Pongo, Missis and Lieutenant Cat enter

Colonel It's exactly as I thought, the Badduns won't be able to see you. And if they do, they'll just think you're some of the dogs they've captured.

Pongo But what about when the television ends?

Colonel Apparently the Badduns just roll over on the floor, and go fast asleep.

Missis Colonel, how do you know about all this?

Colonel Heard it from your boy, Lucky. He's been barking out reports every hour. Good officer material, that pup of yours. I've already made him a corporal.

Missis What, our dear little Lucky?

Lucky Yes, Mother. I'm here, Mother. And so are the others. Evening, Father.

Missis Little Cadpig, Patch and Roly Poly? You're all here?

Much joy

Colonel Now calm down, you lot. They might hear over there.

Missis Quiet as mice.

Lucky (*to the dogs*) Still, tails, still. Be still! (*To the Colonel*) I'm teaching them to obey orders as you suggested, sir.

Colonel Excellent, excellent. I'm promoting you to Sergeant. Carry on this way and I'll commission you next week. Now, I must be off. The Lieutenant and I will make a strategic withdrawal to the perimeter wall and guard your escape route.

Pongo Won't you come and meet the other dogs?

Colonel Not while the Badduns are awake. I don't think even they would mistake me for a Dalmatian. I'll be outside if you need help.

The Colonel exits

There is the distant sound of Cruella de Vil's car-horn

Missis It's lovely and warm.

Pongo There must be more than the fire to keep it so warm.

Lucky There's central heating, too. For when that woman comes to live here. She can't stand being cold.

Missis So that's why everything is painted red.

Pongo It's a bit like being inside a mouth.

Lucky Are you going to help all the dogs to escape, Father?

Pongo I hope so.

Lucky thumps his tail. There is a subdued but positive response

I've been thinking very hard about this and I've decided that the best thing to do is ——

A thunderous knocking at the door. Chaos ensues, as dogs panic and the Badduns lumber to their feet heading for the door

The door is flung open to reveal Cruella de Vil against a moonlit sky

Cruella Saul! Jasper! Turn off that television. And turn on the light.

Saul We've run out of light bulbs.

Jasper And if we turn the telly off there'll be no light at all. It'll be really spooky.

Cruella Well, turn the sound right down. We have things to talk about.

Jasper does so

Saul We might find a light bulb somewhere. I don't suppose you ——

Cruella Don't be ridiculous. I've got a job for you, my lads. Tonight. The dogs must be killed tonight. Every single one of them.

Saul But they're not big enough to be made into fur coats yet.

Cruella The large ones are. The small ones can be made into gloves. Anyway, that's not the point. The point is they have to die before anyone finds them. There's been too much in the newspapers about them; they'll even be on television news tomorrow. All England's looking for the Dearlys' puppies.

Jasper But no-one will find them here.

Saul Why don't we just kill the Dearlys' puppies and let the rest grow until they're big enough?

Cruella Do you know which puppies are the Dearlys'? Have they got different spots or something? Can you really tell the difference?

Saul Well, no.

Jasper Not exackly.

Cruella Someone's bound to hear their daytime barking and tell the police. I've told my husband: he's going to ship the skins abroad. I'll be keeping a few for my own coat. I've decided to make the coat reversible. Dalmatian on the inside and baby seal on the outside.

Jasper
Saul } (*together*) Very nice ...

Cruella We've got a baby seal farm in the Orkneys. Then when all the fuss has died down, we'll start our Dalmatian fur farm up again. That means this lot must be got rid of quickly.

Jasper
Saul } (*together*) But how?

Cruella Any way you like. Poison them; drown them; hit them on the head. Have you any gas? Or any chloroform? I don't care how you do it. Hang them, suffocate them, drop them off the roof, tread on them, smother them with pillows. There are dozens of lovely ways to do the job. If I had the time, I'd do it myself.

Jasper Couldn't you make time, Mrs de Vil?

Saul You'd do it so beautifully. It would be a lesson to us both.

Jasper And such a pleasure to watch.

Cruella I am sorely tempted. No, I have to get back to London. Here's an idea for you. Shut them up in a room without food and then they'll end up killing each other.

Jasper They'd make a horrible noise doing it and we'd never hear the telly.

Saul More important, they would damage each other's skins.

Cruella And that would ruin their value. Quite right, Saul. You must kill them carefully. And you must start to skin them straightaway.

Jasper We can't do that.

Saul What he means is: we don't know how.

Jasper That's what I meant, yeah.

Cruella My husband will show you. We'll both drive down tomorrow night. So they'd better all be dead with their blood drained out by then. And my husband and I will be counting the bodies. If you have let even one of the ninety-seven Dalmatians escape, I'll turn you out of Hell Hall. Now, you'd better get started.

Cruella starts to exit, aiming a kick at a pup on her way out. The pup yelps and other dogs begin to snarl

Good-night and goodbye, you horrid little beasts. You'll be so much better as skins. And I'll simply love those of you who are made into my own new coat. I am really looking forward to that!

Cruella exits

The Badduns shut the door behind her quickly and go into a huddle. We hear the blast of Cruella's car-horn as she drives away

Missis They are going to kill us all. What are we going to do?

Lucky What can I tell the others, Father?

Pongo You have to give me time to think.

Missis If you want to attack those two, you can count on me, Pongo.

Lucky The Badduns always carry knives.

Pongo If we attack them, they may kill us — and then who would there be to help all the others? Let me think.

Jasper No, no, no, no. We can't do it tonight.

Saul Why not?

Jasper We'll miss the telly. It's *What's My Crime?* tonight and we never miss that. It's our favourite programme. We can't miss that. It would be criminal.

Saul Tonight? *What's My Crime?* is on tonight? We'll do it afterwards. While the pups are sleepy. That way, they won't notice and they'll be less dangerous.

Jasper Perhaps we should do it after breakfast. It will take all night, and we'd be exhausted. Then we've got to think about skinning them.

Saul Perhaps we could skin them alive and watch the telly at the same time?

Jasper They'd never keep still. And think about the noise they'd make. And the mess.

Lucky gives three short sharp loud barks

Lucky "Wuff, wuff, wuff?" (*"What's My Crime?"*)

Jasper That's one of them now. I'll kill the little ——

Saul roars. Jasper howls as they realize

Saul
Jasper } (*together*) It's *What's My Crime?*

Saul turns up the sound, Jasper adjusts the picture. They fling themselves down to watch

Pongo Lucky! How long does this television thing last?

Saul
Jasper } (*together*) Ooooh!

Lucky It lasts for half an hour, I think.

Saul
Jasper } (*together*) Aaaah!

Pongo Where does that door lead?

Saul
Jasper } (*together*) Ha, ha, ha!

Lucky It leads to the larder. Where the food's kept.

Saul
Jasper } (*together*) Ummmmm!

Pongo Is there a window? Yes! Then we'll escape through the window. Line them all up.

Saul
Jasper } (*together*) Yessss!

Pongo And make sure they all have a good, quick feed. It's a long way home.

Missis And leave a little for us, please.

Lucky Right, Father. Right, Mother.

Saul
Jasper } (*together*) Go for it!

The dogs begin to leave

Jasper Do you reckon we could ever get on this programme?

Saul What you and me in evening dress with carnations in our buttonholes — and all England watching us? We'd have to do something really original like what he has.

Jasper Why, what's he done?

Saul He was last week's surprise guest. The one that stole two hundred bath plugs from hotels all over the country. Don't you remember?

Jasper That's just silly. What could he do with two hundred bath plugs?

Saul Sell them back to the hotels he stole them from, of course.

Jasper That's about as silly as us taking all these dogs to another place and then selling them back.

Saul Selling them back to who?

Jasper To Mrs High-and-Mighty Cruella de Vil.

Saul That really is silly. Anyway, shut up and watch. No more talking. Understood?

All the dogs leave

Lucky and Pongo are last

Pongo   Ha! Ha!

Lucky and Pongo exit

Pause

Saul What's that noise?

Jasper What noise? There's nothing there.

Saul   ⎱ (*together*) Nothing there? (*They turn and look*) Nothing? Quick!
Jasper ⎰   After them!

SCENE 5

Outside Hell Hall. Night to early morning

The Colonel, Lieutenant Cat, Pongo, Missis and Lucky enter

Colonel All safely in the barn, Lieutenant?

Lieutenant Cat Yes, sir!

Missis Pongo, did you manage to bolt the larder door behind you?

Pongo Absolutely. Those bolts aren't good for the teeth, though.

Colonel Good decision to leave. I'm promoting Lucky to Sergeant-Major. All the others have been taken to a barn for a good sleep ready for the morning. We'll arrange everything at Dawn Barking. Now, what about you three? Time for a bit of shut-eye for you as well. Follow me. Lieutenant!

Lieutenant Cat Miaou?

Colonel You keep watch. Any funny business and let me know. The usual way. Right?

Lieutenant Cat The usual way. Right!

Lieutenant Cat hides behind/in a tree

Colonel Now come on you three.

The Colonel, Pongo, Missis, and Lucky exit. Lanterns are seen swinging and searching as the Badduns enter

Jasper Over here! Over here!

Saul What have you found?

Jasper Nothing. That's what I was saying. There's nothing over here.

Saul This is going to take all night. Just carry on searching, Jasper.

Saul and Jasper resume searching

Jasper (*stopping*) Saul!

Saul Yes, Jasper.

Jasper Just tell me again what we're looking for. Refresh me memory.

Saul That'll be the day. We're looking for lots of pawprints. All those dogs must have left their pawmarks somewhere. Pawprints. Right?

Jasper Pawprince, yeah. Here, Pawprince. Pretty Pawprince. Here Prince.

Lieutenant Cat howls a warning miaou. Jasper jumps

What on earth was that? Was that a Pawprince?
Saul No, Jasper, it was a cat howling at the moon or something. Just keep
on searching. Pawprints, right?
Jasper Pawprince, right!

The Colonel enters and sees the Badduns

Colonel "Now, let slip the dogs of war!"

*The Colonel attacks the Badduns. He eventually bites both brothers in the
legs*

Saul and Jasper howl, drop their lanterns and run off limping

Lieutenant Cat Good work, Colonel.
Colonel Good watchkeeping, Lieutenant. I'm promoting you to Captain.
Lieutenant Cat Why thank you, Colonel.
Colonel Nothing at all, really. I've just made myself Brigadier-General.
Now, it'll soon be dawn. Follow me, Captain.

Lieutenant/Captain Cat and Colonel/Brigadier-General exit

Dawn reveals a distant village

Pongo, Missis, and Lucky enter

Missis If we march on like this it won't be long before we are home. Now
what was it the Colonel said?
Pongo Look out for a village and smell out the bakery. The dog-baker will
make sure we can get all the food we want.

Lucky skips ahead

Missis Then all we need is plenty of water — and we can carry on all day.
Pongo Remember the humans. And the police. We must hide by day and
travel by night.
Missis Where's Lucky?
Pongo I thought he was with you.
Missis I thought he was with you.

Lucky enters, covered in black

Ask that nice little pup over there.

Pongo Pup? A black pup? A stranger? Who are you, my lad? Where have you come from?

Lucky does not answer. He butts Missis in the stomach in a friendly way

Missis Goodness. Lucky. It is Lucky. What are you doing in that soot bag? You need a good wash right away. Come here at once.

Lucky I was at the chimney-sweep's house in the village and I got stuck in this bag of soot. Sorry!

Pongo It's all right, Missis. He's given me an idea. Lucky, were there a lot of soot bags at the sweep's?

Lucky There were bags and bags and bags.

Pongo Then we are all going to turn into black dogs. That way no human will know who are we are or what we are. We can travel by day and be invisible by night.

Missis What a brilliant idea. You are a genius, Pongo.

Pongo (*embarrassed*) So let's go and make sure that everyone is made sootably ready!

All exit laughing

Evening. The distant sound of Cruella's car-horn

Saul and Jasper enter. An opportunity for some work in the audience!

Saul They're around here somewhere.

Jasper How do you know, Saul?

Saul I can smell 'em.

Jasper I can't see any dog — wait a minute! Yes, I can. There's a dog running out of the village. But it's not one of ours.

Saul Are you sure?

Jasper Course I'm sure. The dog's all black. Not a touch of white on it. No, it's not one of ours.

The sound of the car-horn

Saul Oh, no, there she is now. Well, we'd better carry on searching or she'll skin us, not the dogs. They'll be heading for London, so let's go that way.

Jasper Which way?

Saul That way.

Saul and Jasper exit

The sound of a lorry-horn. A black removal lorry becomes visible and stops. We hear the engine turn off, and a door slam on the driver's side

Billie, the driver, comes to the rear of the lorry

Billie Out yer comes, Bull. Stay yere and mind the van. I forgot something for the kids. I won't be long.

The rear of the lorry opens and out hops a Staffordshire Terrier with what looks like a clay pipe in his mouth. He pulls out a newspaper and starts to read it. Billie exits. Pongo, Missis and Lucky enter, apparently members of the New Zealand Rugby team

Pongo I was definitely last out of the village.

Missis And she was there?

Pongo Cruella de Vil is hot on our tails. I saw her clearly. We have to go this way, now. Her car was blocking the proper way to London. We would never have got the puppies past them all. As it was I nearly got caught.

The sound of Cruella de Vil's car-horn in the distance

Missis It's her. She's on her way.

Pongo The Badduns won't be far behind. And they've been told to kill us all.

Missis What do we do now?

Pongo Only a miracle can save us now.

Missis Then we must find a miracle. Pongo, what's a miracle?

The horn sounds again, closer

Lucky Perhaps that Terrier can help us.

Missis Terriers are good guard and watch dogs — but they're always a bit reserved.

Lucky What does that mean?

Missis It means they keep themselves to themselves and aren't too good at helping.

Pongo But we have to try. Terrier! We need help. We are being pursued by a wicked woman and some wicked men. There are ninety-nine of us. Dalmatians. In disguise. Where can we hide off this road?

The Terrier drops his newspaper

Terrier I don't know, mite. I'm a stranger 'ere myself. My pet's juss driven dahn from Lunnon. Dalmatians, eh? I've 'eard abaht you on the Barkin's. An' I've juss bin' readin' abaht yer in the paper. Ninety-nine of yer,eh? Yer'd better hide in my pet's lorry. The back's open. When the wicked woman 'as gawn past, yer can all get aht an' carry on.

Pongo Missis, that is a miracle. Lucky, tell the other pups, immediately.

Lucky exits

The horn sounds ever closer

Missis So that's what a miracle is — a kind of big, black lorry.

Terrier Lucky the lorry was empty. Who's arter you, mates? Old Nick 'isself?

Pongo Certainly a relation of his. And she's on her way here now.

Pongo has heard the horn sound again and seen headlights

Dogs are pouring into the back of the lorry. Lucky is hushing them

See those headlights? She's in that car. I've made a terrible mistake. Her headlights will shine into the back of your lorry.

Terrier That's a very good point, mite. 'Er lights will shine in the back.

Pongo So what can we do? She will see everything. Can we shut the tailgate?

Terrier Shut ver tilegate. That would do it. Yeah!

Pongo Well let's do it, then.

Terrier Nah! We can't shut ver tilegate.

Pongo Why in dogbasket not?

Terrier 'Cos it tikes a newman ter shut ver tilegate. But don't you worry. She won't see black dogs in a black lorry. Not if they all close their eyes.

Pongo Missis! Go and tell the pups to close their eyes. Tell them not to be frightened — just to keep their eyes and their muzzles shut until I give the word. Quickly, Missis.

Missis heads for and into the lorry

The headlights are getting brighter and brighter, the car nearer and nearer

And remember to close your own eyes, Missis!

Terrier You too, mate. Oh, blimey — too late. Run fer cover, run fer cover!

Cruella's car screeches to a halt

Cruella, Jasper and Saul enter

They start to search around. Jasper looks in the back of the lorry and sees nothing. Cruella and Saul nearly discover Pongo, but are distracted by the Terrier and by the entrance of Billie, the lorry-driver

Cruella Badduns! You two lost them. You can find them.
Billie Sumfin' yer wants?
Cruella We're searching for some dogs.
Billie 'E's not fer sile.
Cruella You misunderstand. They are our dogs we are looking for. I wouldn't want him.
Billie An' why not? You got sumfin' against 'im, missis?

Jasper smells a fight, and begins to take up a pose. Saul is heading for the back of the lorry

Jasper You got something against us?
Saul
Jasper } (*together*) Yeah? Yeah? Yeah?
Billie Yeah! An' 'e can keep 'is nose out er my van. *Bull!*
Saul Mrs de Vil! Mrs de Vil!

The Terrier attacks Saul; Billie thumps Jasper

The Badduns run away. Cruella flounces off and drives away hooting in anger

Billie Right, Bull. Well done, mate. I dunno wot she were arter. but we ain't got it. Off home back to Lunnon nah, eh? It's nearly Christmas, and time we was seein' if you've got any presents.

Billie exits to start up the lorry, leaving the tailgate down

Pongo emerges from hiding

Pongo Missis was absolutely right. You are a miracle.
Terrier Dalmatians, eh? I met a Dalmatian once. He lives quite close to me. Handsome looking cove he is — with a very distinct mark on his muzzle like a pair of dumb-bells.
Pongo Dumb-bell on his muzzle?
Terrier Nice dog, but lonely. 'E'd lost his wife, summ'ow. 'Ere, do you want a lift back to Lunnon? We were going back empty, anyway.
Pongo Yes, we would like a lift back to London, thank you. How many days will it take?

Terrier My pet's not vat bad a driver. It'll tike — oh, a couple of ahrs. Billie'll wanna get 'ome an' decorate the Christmas tree. So tell yer pups when ve driver comes back ter put ver tailboard up, keep quiet, and shut veir eyes again. Come on, mite, less go an' tell 'em what ter do. Ven you kin tell me orl abaht yer adventures. I'm longin' ter 'ear abaht vem.

Pongo And I want to hear about this Dalmatian with the dumb-bell marking.

Pongo and the Terrier head for the back of the lorry and get inside. Billie enters and heads for the tail of the lorry

Billie Bull! Where are yer? I'm always forgettin' to shut the tail up. Spesherly when we're empty. Where's that Canine Cannon Bull of mine. There you are. Stayin' inside to keep warm, is it? Right you are, Bull. (*He puts up the tailboard*) Next stop, St John's Wood. Home in time for Christmas. Christmas in Lunnon. Lunnon at Christmas. That's the spirit!

Billie goes round to the front of the lorry

We hear a door slam, the engine start, and the lorry drive off. Cruella's car-horn sounds, quite close, as she drives up

Cruella enters

Cruella Saul! Jasper! I'm sure I left you somewhere near here. Badduns! *Badduns!* We have to have a talk. Where are my poor boys? I've come to take you home. Now boys, all is forgiven. We'll find those dogs soon — it'll take them days to walk or even run back to London. Days and days. Somebody's bound to see them and tell the Dearlys and they'll tell me. We three must go back to Hell Hall. Sharpen the knives, and empty all the buckets, and tidy everything up. And when they've finished tidying up Hell Hall, I will tidy those two up. Nobody fails Cruella de Vil. Nobody. First the Hall and then London!

Cruella exits

The car is heard driving off

SCENE 6

Outside Cruella de Vil's house. Night

Cruella's Persian Cat is in hiding

Pongo, Missis, and Lucky enter

Pongo Tell the puppies to stop, Lucky. We're nearly home.

Lucky Can I tell them exactly where we are?

Pongo Yes. That is our enemy's house. Cruella de Vil's London house.

Missis If we could only get inside it, we could attack it.

Lucky May we attack it? Please, please.

Missis You would only hurt your nails and teeth.

Persian Cat (*in a slightly foreign accent*) Miaou. I think I have to surrender. There are too many of you.

Pongo Madam Cat, none of us would ever think of hurting you.

Persian Cat What a civil speech! That's the civillest speech I've ever heard from a dog. Who are you? There are no black dogs around here.

Pongo We are not usually black except for our spots.

Persian Cat Now I know exactly who you are. You rescued all the dogs from Hell Hall! Bravo! Well done! I couldn't be more pleased.

Missis Why should you, a city cat, be pleased? And how do you know about Hell Hall? Is your pet by any chance Cruella de Vil?

Persian Cat Yes, she is. Cruella de Vil — the cruel devil.

Missis And she drowns all your kittens.

Persian Cat She does. Forty-four she has drowned so far. Would you dogs care to come in to the house and do some damage now?

Lucky Oh, please, let us.

Puppies Please, oh please.

Pongo Isn't Cruella at home?

Persian Cat No, she went back to Hell Hall. Oh do come in and do some damage. It would be such fun. For all of us.

The dogs are led into Cruella's by the Persian Cat. They destroy her furs (of which there are rooms full), her ermine sheets, et cetera and cause what looks like a snowstorm. The sound of Cruella's car-horn

The noise of the dogs at work is silenced, as they disappear. Cruella enters in her white mink. She goes to her front door and tries to unlock it. As she bends forward, Pongo, Missis and Lucky appear from behind the house. They rip off her white mink coat and run off

Cruella My best mink! It's bewitched! I must tell the police. (*She turns back to the door, unlocks it*)

The front door swings open to release a cloud of choking fur

My God! What's happened? All my lovely furs. They're ruined. Ruined. Help, help. Somebody call the police. How can I live without my furs. I'll freeze to death. It's the end of everything. Everything. Don't you laugh at me. Don't you dare laugh at me. Do you know who I am? I am Cruella de Vil —— Cruella de Vil and you are just horrid. All of you: horrid. So I'm not going to stay with you any more. See. You'll just see.

Cruella goes inside crying

SCENE 7

The Dearlys' dining-room

A decorated Christmas tree

Mrs Dearly and Nanny Cook are trying to be festive. Perdita is present

Mrs Dearly Christmas Day, tomorrow. Turkey and presents, I'm really looking forward to it. It's a beautiful Christmas tree, Nanny Cook.

Nanny Cook Thank you, ma'am. It's begun to snow. Heavily, this time. And Missis didn't even take her blue coat.

Mrs Dearly Don't talk about the dogs. Let's sing a carol.

Nanny Cook Won't that be a bit sad?

Mrs Dearly It just seems proper on Christmas Eve.

They sing "Silent Night"

Nanny Cook That was sad. What do you suggest now?

Mrs Dearly We could play Snap, Beggar-My-Neighbour, or Animal Grab. Until Mr Dearly comes home from his important meeting.

Nanny Cook Isn't it just like the Government to call an important meeting on Christmas Eve?

A dog barks outside

Mrs Dearly That sounded just like Pongo.

Nanny Cook goes to the window. Another dog barks

And that sounded just like Missis.

Nanny Cook (*from the window*) The dogs are black, madam.

Mrs Dearly Tell them they shouldn't be out on a night like this. Tell them to go home to their owner.

Mrs Dearly moves to the window. The dogs bark again. Perdita gets very excited and runs for the door and howls at it

There's something strange going on. I recognized their voices. You recognized their voices. And so does Perdita. Go out and have a look. (*She goes towards the door*)

Nanny Cook I think it's just wishful thinking.

Mrs Dearly Well we can check their collars, anyway. That should tell us where they come from. And where to take them back.

The door bursts open and Pongo, Missis and what seems like a flood of Dalmatians (properly accoutred in white and black spots) enter

Jubilation

This is wonderful. You said they were all black.

Nanny Cook The snow must have washed the black away.

Mrs Dearly And how many are there of them?

Nanny Cook I've lost count.

Pongo Woofty-woof.

Mrs Dearly However many, they will all need a home.

Nanny Cook Well, the drawing-room is very large. I've always thought so.

Mrs Dearly Pongo! I'm going to start listening to you more closely, my lad. Where have you all been?

Pongo Wuffolk!

Mrs Dearly Let me think. Wuffolk. Suffolk! Hasn't Cruella de Vil got a big house there? She mentioned it at dinner that night. Oh, Nanny Cook. Isn't it wonderful?

Mr Dearly enters in outdoor clothes

Mr Dearly So that's why there are so many Dalmatians in the house. Missis. Pongo.

Pongo and Missis greet him effusively

Just be quiet everyone and listen to me. There are such goings on at the de Vils' house. Somebody got in there and destroyed Mr de Vil's whole stock of furs. Mrs de Vil's going around screaming that it's the end of everything.

Mrs Dearly Why should it be the end of everything?

Mr Dearly Because most of the furs weren't paid for.

Mrs Dearly So de Vil is ruined.

Mr Dearly So is his wife. And they're leaving England tonight to get away from all their debts. She looks awful. The black side of hair has gone white. And the white side's gone a horrid shade of green! So that's her finished.

Mrs Dearly I'm not so sure about that.

Nanny Cook Now, we've got all these dogs to feed. We'd better start straight away.

Mrs Dearly Will any shops still be open, do you think?

Mr Dearly Probably not on Christmas Eve, my dear. But I've had an idea. I was on a Committttee with someone who might be able to help. Come on, everyone. Let's go and get organized.

Nanny Cook and Mr and Mrs Dearly exit

Perdita This is wonderful. You must tell me everything.

Pongo We will, we will.

Perdita You go out to find fifteen puppies and bring back hundreds.

Missis Ninety-seven actually.

Perdita And with us that makes ninety-eight, ninety-nine, one hundred. Just think, one hundred Dalmatians!

Pongo There's one more.

Perdita One more? Who's that?

Missis The one you fell in love with.

Perdita The Dalmatian I love?

Pongo That's him.

Perdita How in dogbasket have you found him?

Missis Well, it's all part of the adventure — but we met a Staffordshire Terrier who knew him and who's going to bring him here.

Pongo So that will make us all ——

All — one hundred and one Dalmatians.

CURTAIN

FURNITURE AND PROPERTY LIST

ACT I

Prologue

On stage: Parcels (for **Mrs Dearly**)

Scene 1

On stage: Dining-table
Chairs
Butler's table. *On it*: telephone, cutlery for 3, folded tablecloth
Carpet

Personal: **Cruella de Vil**: ropes of pearls

Scene 2

On stage: White marble dining-table. *On it*: 3 place settings, 3 soup bowls, 3
plates
Fur hangings on walls, etc.
3 chairs
Sideboard. *On it*: gong

Off stage: Soup tureen with ladle (**Servant 1**)
Plate of bright green fish (**Servant 2**)
Blue meat joint on covered meat dish, carvers (**Servant 3**)
Dish of black "ice-cream" with serving spoon (**Servant 4**)
Suitcases (**Servants**)
Suitcase (**James**)

Scene 3

On stage: Dining-table. *On it*: tablecloth
Chairs
Butler's table. *On it*: telephone
Carpet

SCENE 4

On stage: As previous scene

Off stage: Broom (**Nanny Cook**)

ACT II

SCENE 1

On stage: Broken down stage-coach. *In it*: straw, two chops, cakes, box of chocolates
A light motor-cycle with a sidecar

Off stage: Stone (**Child**)

SCENE 2

On stage: Fireplace
Chair
Table. *On it*: silver kettle boiling above a spirit lamp, plate with slices of bread and silver cover, butter dish, dish of cakes, cup, saucer, silver bowl, milk jug, knife, toasting fork

Personal: **Saul**: piece of paper in pocket

SCENE 3

On stage: Tree

SCENE 4

On stage: TV
Firegrate

SCENE 5

On stage: Nil

Off stage: Lanterns (**Saul**, **Jasper**)
Rear of lorry

Personal: **Terrier**: clay pipe, newspaper

On stage: Furs

Off stage: Fur debris (**Stage Management**)

Personal: **Cruella**: doorkey

SCENE 7

On stage: Dining-table. *On it*: tablecloth
                 Chairs
                 Butler's table. *On it*: telephone
                 Carpet
                 Decorated Christmas tree

LIGHTING PLOT

Practical fittings required: TV for Act II, Scene 4
Various interior and exterior settings

ACT I

To open: General exterior late afternoon light on Park area

Cue 1	The **Dearlys** approach the car *Cross-fade to the* **Dearlys** *dining-room*	(Page 1)
Cue 2	**Pongo** and **Mr Dearly** exit *Cross-fade to broom cupboard*	(Page 10)
Cue 3	**Pongo**: "Now what about these two?" *Cross-fade to exterior light with impending storm effect*	(Page 10)
Cue 4	To open SCENE 2 *Cross-fade to* **de Vil**'s *dining-room*	(Page 11)
Cue 5	**Cruella**: " ... time for the Badduns." *Cross-fade to exterior late evening light with storm effect*	(Page 14)
Cue 6	To open SCENE 3 *Gloomy daylight interior on the* **Dearlys** *dining-room*	(Page 15)
Cue 7	**Pongo** and **Perdita** exit *Fade to black-out; when ready, bring up afternoon interior lighting on the* **Dearlys** *dining-room*	(Page 20)

ACT II

To open: Exterior daylight

Cue 8	Sound of a van driving off *Cross-fade to Sudbury Manor interior with fireglow*	(Page 33)
Cue 9	**Sir Charles**: " ... after all these years." *Cross-fade to cloudy moonlight on Hell Hall exterior*	(Page 36)

Cue 10	**Lieutenant Cat**: " ... the Colonel now."	(Page 37)
	Begin gradual cross-fade to early morning light	
Cue 11	The **Colonel**, **Missis** and **Pongo** exit	(Page 38)
	Cross-fade to firelight and TV flicker on kitchen interior; moonlight outside door	
Cue 12	**Saul** and **Jasper**: "After them!"	(Page 44)
	Cross-fade to night light on Hell Hall exterior; gradually bringing up dawn effect as scene progresses	
Cue 13	All exit laughing	(Page 46)
	Change to evening light; gradually dimming to night	
Cue 14	**Pongo**: " ... her way here now."	(Page 48)
	Car headlights approaching	
Cue 15	**Missis** gets into the back of the lorry	(Page 49)
	Car headlights getting brighter	
Cue 16	Car drives away	(Page 49)
	Car headlights recede	
Cue 17	Lorry drives off	(Page 50)
	Car headlights approaching	
Cue 18	Car is heard driving off	(Page 50)
	*Headlights receding; cross-fade to night light on **de Vil**'s house exterior*	
Cue 19	**Persian Cat**: "For all of us."	(Page 51)
	Bring up light on interior	
Cue 20	**Cruella** goes inside crying	(Page 52)
	*Cross-fade to the **Dearlys** dining-room*	

EFFECTS PLOT

ACT I

Cue 14	**Nanny Cook**: " ... real scamps." *Doorbell*	(Page 20)
Cue 15	**Nanny Cook**: " ... at a terrific speed." *Strident car-horn twice*	(Page 21)
Cue 16	**Mr Dearly**: "Just listen!" *Bark message as script page 25, repeated in distance*	(Page 25)
Cue 17	**Mr** and **Mrs Dearly** exit *Deep, distant bark-message*	(Page 25)
Cue 18	**Nanny Cook** goes to sit down *Telephone*	(Page 26)

ACT II

Cue 19	**Pongo** and **Missis** and the **Spaniel** exit *Car driving off; motor-cycle arriving*	(Page 32)
Cue 20	The **Badduns** drive off *Motor-cycle driving off*	(Page 33)
Cue 21	**Pongo** and **Missis** and the **Spaniel** exit *Thunderous knocking at front door*	(Page 35)
Cue 22	**Jasper** approaches **Sir Charles** *Door slam*	(Page 35)
Cue 23	To open SCENE 4 *TV sound*	(Page 38)
Cue 24	The **Colonel** exits *Distant strident car-horn*	(Page 39)
Cue 25	**Pongo**: " ...the best thing to do is ——" *Thunderous knocking at door*	(Page 40)
Cue 26	**Jasper** turns off the TV sound *Cut TV sound*	(Page 40)
Cue 27	The **Badduns** go into a huddle *Strident car-horn*	(Page 42)
Cue 28	**Saul** turns up the sound *Bring up TV sound*	(Page 42)

Cue 29	All exit laughing *Strident car-horn*	(Page 46)
Cue 30	**Jasper**: " ... not one of ours." *Strident car-horn*	(Page 46)
Cue 31	**Saul** and **Jasper** exit *Lorry horn; lorry engine stops; door slam*	(Page 46)
Cue 32	**Pongo**: " ... I nearly got caught." *Strident car-horn in distance*	(Page 47)
Cue 33	**Missis**: " ... what's a miracle?" *Strident car-horn nearer*	(Page 47)
Cue 34	**Lucky** exits *Strident car-horn closer*	(Page 48)
Cue 35	**Pongo**: " ... on her way here now." *Strident car-horn closer*	(Page 48)
Cue 36	**Missis** gets into the lorry *Car engine getting nearer*	(Page 48)
Cue 37	**Terrier**: " ... run fer cover!" *Car screeches to a halt*	(Page 48)
Cue 38	**Cruella** flounces off. Short pause *Strident car-horn; car drawing away*	(Page 49)
Cue 39	**Billie** goes round to the front of the lorry *Door slam; lorry engine starts and drives off; strident car-horn, car approaching and stopping*	(Page 50)
Cue 40	**Cruella** exits *Car driving off*	(Page 50)
Cue 41	The dogs destroy the furs. Snowstorm *Strident car-horn*	(Page 51)